EDGE OF EXTINCTION

TIGERS

TRICIA HOFFMAN

PowerKiDS press

Published in 2027 by The Rosen Publishing Group, Inc.
2544 Clinton Street, Buffalo, NY 14224

First Edition

Portions of this work were originally authored by Michael Portman and published as *Animals At Risk: Tigers in Danger*. All new material in this edition is authored by Tricia Hoffman.

Editor: Tricia Hoffman
Book Design: Beeline Media and Design

Photo Credits: Cover, p. 1 NNER/Shutterstock.com; p. 4 Eric Isselee/Shutterstock.com; p. 5 DSlight_photography/Shutterstock.com; p. 7 Dekajhon/Shutterstock.com; p. 9 GUDKOV ANDREY/Shutterstock.com; p. 11 Jake Oneill/Shutterstock.com; p. 13 Deepankar90/Shutterstock.com; p. 14 Rob Crandall/Shutterstock.com; p. 15 Lauren Bilboe/Shutterstock.com; p. 17 Anuradha Marwah/Shutterstock.com; p. 19 Thanumporn Thongkongkaew/Shutterstock.com; p. 21 Steve Cukrov/Shutterstock.com; p. 21 Piotr Swat/Shutterstock.com; p. 21 Photoongraphy/Shutterstock.com; p. 21 Duski Saad/Shutterstock.com

Cataloging-in-Publication Data
Names: Hoffman, Tricia.
Title: Tigers / Tricia Hoffman.
Description: Buffalo, New York : PowerKids Press, 2027. | Series: Edge of extinction | Includes glossary and index.
Identifiers: ISBN 9781499457957 (pbk.) | ISBN 9781499457964 (library bound) | ISBN 9781499457971 (ebook)
Subjects: LCSH: Tiger--Juvenile literature. | Tiger--Conservation--Juvenile literature. | Endangered species--Juvenile literature.
Classification: LCC QL737.C23 H644 2027 | DDC 599.756--dc23

Printed in China

CPSIA Compliance Information: Batch #QSPK27. For Further Information contact Rosen Publishing at 1-800-237-9932.

Contents

Words in the glossary appear in **bold** type the first time they are used in the text.

The World's Largest Cats

Tigers are known for their orange and white fur with black stripes. Their strength and beauty have made them both loved and feared. Different kinds of tigers live in different **habitats**, some cold and snowy, and others hot and rainy. However, all tigers like to be in forested areas.

Tigers are the largest cat **species** in the world. But these beautiful beasts face serious **threats** because of **poaching** and habitat loss. Tigers are at risk of becoming **extinct** and dying out completely.

Tigers are good swimmers. They often swim to cool off in hot weather.

Six Subspecies

There are six types, or subspecies, of tigers left in the world. Amur tigers are the largest tigers. Males can be up to 10 feet (3 m) long and 660 pounds (300 kg). They mostly live in the forests of eastern Russia, though some have been found in China and North Korea. The smallest tiger is the Sumatran. Most adult males are about 3 feet (2.4 m) long and weigh about 220 pounds (100 kg).

Bengal tigers are the most common type. India has the largest population. The Indochinese, Malayan, and South China tigers live in several Asian countries. All six subspecies are **endangered**.

ON THE EDGE

Just 100 years ago, there were nine subspecies of tigers. Since then, the Caspian, Javan, and Bali tigers have all gone extinct.

A tiger's stripes are unique, like a human fingerprint.

Time for Lunch

Tigers are fierce predators. They are carnivores, which means they only eat meat. They hunt turtles, frogs, deer, pigs, birds, and even baby elephants. If there is leftover meat from a big kill, the tiger will cover it with leaves and dirt. When it's hungry again, it comes back to feed. Sometimes they will share a large meal with other tigers.

Tigers are usually nocturnal, which means they sleep during the day and hunt at night. They have excellent eyesight and can see well in the dark. Tigers' stripes act as **camouflage**, making it hard for other animals to spot them.

ON THE EDGE

An adult tiger can eat up to 60 pounds (27 kg) of meat a day.

Tigers are ambush predators. That means they catch prey by surprise.

Tiger Territories

Tigers need large amounts of food in order to **survive**. A forest that has a lot of animals is a good habitat because each tiger is able to find plenty of food.

In Russian forests, where there are few animals, tigers have large territories because they must travel long distances in search of food. In India, where there are many animals, a tiger's territory is often much smaller.

Tigers like to live and hunt alone. A male tiger will protect his territory from other males. But he may share it with female tigers.

ON THE EDGE

Tigers will mark their territory with their scent and scratch marks on trees.

A tiger's roar can be heard as far as 2 miles (3.2 km) away.

Habitat Loss

One of the biggest threats tigers face today is habitat loss. Large areas of tigers' forest habitats have been cleared for lumber and to make room for homes and farms. Tigers that once had large territories must now live in much smaller areas.

Many tigers live close to people. This has caused problems for both people and tigers. People hunt many of the same animals that tigers eat. Without enough food, hungry tigers attack farm animals instead of their usual prey. Farmers may kill tigers to protect their own animals.

ON THE EDGE

Not all tigers are orange and black. Bengal tigers have brown stripes instead of black. Golden tigers have golden fur with cinnamon-colored stripes.

Tigers' habitats are 93 percent smaller than they once were.

Illegal Hunting

Poaching is another big threat facing tigers today. For hundreds of years, killing a tiger was a sign of bravery. Many people wanted tiger meat, skin, bones, and other body parts as well.

In China, tiger bones have been used in **medicines** for more than 1,000 years. Tiger skins are used for clothing and decorations. Claws, teeth, and whiskers are sometimes used as good-luck charms.

Although these activities are now illegal, poaching continues. At least 150 tigers are killed by poachers each year.

The front teeth of a tiger can be 3 inches (7.6 cm) long. They were once used to treat toothaches.

Mothers and Cubs

Female tigers have three or four cubs every two years. Tiger cubs are born blind and weigh just 2 to 3 pounds (0.9 to 1.4 kg). They depend on their mother for everything. Mother tigers raise their cubs alone. Fathers leave before the cubs are born.

Cubs usually can't survive on their own until they're about two years old. Cubs younger than this can die from lack of food. When a poacher kills a tiger, the loss may be more than just one animal. If a female tiger, or tigress, is raising cubs, killing her may result in the death of the entire family.

ON THE EDGE

Tiger cubs left unguarded can also become prey for other animals, even other tigers.

The mother tiger teaches her cubs hunting skills through play.

Protecting Tiger Habitats

A healthy tiger population depends on the tigers' habitat. To save wild tigers, their forest and jungle habitats throughout Asia must be protected. Tigers must also be protected from poachers.

Today, governments and wildlife groups are working together to solve these problems. **Nature reserves** have been created to keep tigers safe. Governments are also working hard to stop the illegal trade of tiger parts. However, more reserves need to be built and stronger laws against poaching must be put into effect. The future of tigers depends on it.

ON THE EDGE

Tigers raised in zoos usually cannot be freed into the wild. They don't have the skills to survive on their own.

Climate change has a negative impact on tigers as well. Without a supply of food and clean water, tigers cannot survive.

Save the Tigers!

Luckily, tiger populations are showing slow signs of recovery. In 2010, numbers were at an all-time low of 3,200 tigers in the wild. Now, scientists **estimate** there are more than 5,500. Even though tiger numbers are increasing in some areas, tiger habitats continue to decrease. Some groups are working to help with this.

It's a long road, but everyone can work together to make sure tiger populations can continue to grow. And that means you can help too!

ON THE EDGE

Tigers can live to be more than 20 years old in zoos but usually only live about 15 years in the wild.

What Can You Do to Help?

International Tiger Day is July 29th. Make posters on this day to teach people about the dangers that tigers face.

Save energy. You can help prevent climate change by turning off lights when you leave the room and taking short showers.

Read labels. Tiger habitats are being destroyed to plant more oil palm trees. Buy products that use sustainable palm oil to avoid cutting down more forests.

Adopt a tiger through the World Wildlife Fund. Donate money that will go toward creating reserves for tigers, protection from poachers, and other conservation work.

Glossary

camouflage: a color or pattern that matches surroundings and helps an animal hide

endangered: in danger of dying out

estimate: a guess based on knowledge or facts

extinct: having no living members

habitat: an area where plants, animals, and other living things live

medicine: a drug used to treat an illness

nature reserve: a safe area for endangered animals

poaching: illegal hunting

prey: an animal that is hunted by another animal for food

species: a group of animals that are all of the same kind

survive: to stay alive

threat: something likely to cause harm

Fact Check

1. Tigers are the largest ________ species in the world.
   a. endangered b. cat c. canine
2. All tigers like to be in ________ areas.
   a. cold b. warm c. forested
3. What is the most common type of tiger?
   a. Bengal b. Sumatran c. Amur

Answers: 1. b, 2. c, 3. a

On the Internet

Tiger
www.worldwildlife.org/species/finder/tigers/
Read facts about several subspecies of tigers.

Tigers
https://kids.nationalgeographic.com/animals/mammals/facts/tiger
Watch videos, hear sounds, and see pictures of tigers.

Publisher's note to educators and parents: Our editors have carefully reviewed these websites to ensure that they are suitable for students. Many websites change frequently, however, and we cannot guarantee that a site's future contents will continue to meet our high standards of quality and educational value. Be advised that students should be closely supervised whenever they access the Internet.

Index